Short Stories for Students, Volume 13

Staff

Editor: Jennifer Smith.

Contributing Editors: Anne Marie Hacht, Michael L. LaBlanc, Ira Mark Milne, Elizabeth Thomason, Carol Ullmann.

Managing Editor, Content: Dwayne D. Hayes.

Managing Editor, Product: David Galens.

Publisher, Literature Product: Mark Scott.

Literature Content Capture: Joyce Nakamura, *Managing Editor.* Michelle Kazensky, *Associate Editor.*

Research: Victoria B. Cariappa, *Research Manager.* Cheryl Warnock, *Research Specialist.* Sarah Genik, Ron Morelli, Tamara Nott, Tracie A. Richardson, *Research Associates.* Nicodemus Ford, *Research Assistant.*

Permissions: Maria Franklin, *Permissions Manager.* Kim Davis, *Permissions Associate.*

Manufacturing: Mary Beth Trimper, *Manager, Composition and Electronic Prepress.* Evi Seoud, *Assistant Manager, Composition Purchasing and Electronic Prepress.* Stacy Melson, *Buyer.*

Imaging and Multimedia Content Team: Barbara Yarrow, *Manager.* Randy Bassett, *Imaging Supervisor.* Robert Duncan, Dan Newell, *Imaging Specialists.* Pamela A. Reed, *Imaging Coordinator.* Leitha Etheridge-Sims, Mary Grimes, David G. Oblender, *Image Catalogers.* Robyn V. Young, *Project Manager.* Dean Dauphinais, *Senior Image Editor.* Kelly A. Quin, *Image Editor.*

Product Design Team: Kenn Zorn, *Product Design Manager.* Pamela A. E. Galbreath, *Senior Art Director.* Michael Logusz, *Graphic Artist.*

Copyright Notice

Since this page cannot legibly accommodate all copyright notices, the acknowledgments constitute an extension of the copyright notice.

While every effort has been made to secure permission to reprint material and to ensure the reliability of the information presented in this publication, Gale neither guarantees the accuracy of the data contained herein nor assumes any responsibility for errors, omissions, or discrepancies. Gale accepts no payment for listing; and inclusion in the publication of any organization, agency, institution, publication, service, or individual does not imply endorsement of the editors or publisher. Errors brought to the attention of the publisher and verified to the satisfaction of the publisher will be corrected in future editions.

This publication is a creative work fully protected by all applicable copyright laws, as well as by misappropriation, trade secret, unfair competition, and other applicable laws. The authors and editors of this work have added value to the underlying factual material herein through one or more of the following: unique and original selection, coordination, expression, arrangement, and classification of the information.

All rights to this publication will be vigorously defended.

Copyright © 2001
The Gale Group
27500 Drake Road
Farmington Hills, MI 48331–3535

All rights reserved including the right of reproduction in whole or in part in any form.

ISBN 0-7876-4265-7
ISSN 1092-7735

Printed in the United States of America.
10 9 8 7 6 5 4 3 2 1

This Way for the Gas, Ladies and Gentlemen

Tadeusz Borowski 1946

Introduction

In his introduction to the English translation of *This Way for the Gas, Ladies and Gentleman,* Jan Kott writes of Tadeusz Borowski's decision to render his Auschwitz stories in the first person: "The identification of the author with the narrator was the moral decision of a prisoner who had lived through Auschwitz—an acceptance of mutual responsibility, mutual participation, and mutual guilt for the concentration camp." Indeed, in a review for another author's book about the concentration camps, Borowski stated, "It is impossible to write about Auschwitz impersonally." He defined as the "first duty of Auschwitzers . . . to make clear just what camp is." It is where survival depended on a prisoner's taking part in the murder and degradation of their fellow victims. "But write that you, you were the ones who did this," Borowski intoned. "That a portion of the sad fame of Auschwitz belongs to you as well."

In the collection's title story, Borowski squarely fulfills his obligation. Seen through the eyes of a Polish gentile prisoner, as Borowski himself was, "This Way for the Gas, Ladies and Gentleman" describes a typical day at Auschwitz. The narrator joins in the task of unloading thousands of Jews from the cattle cars and sending them to their death in the gas chamber, all to acquire food and maybe a pair of shoes. Subject matter aside, Borowski's story is chilling and unforgettable in the success with which the narrator distances himself from his actions. As readers grow to understand that the narrator is forced to this extreme in order to continue to perform the work that guarantees his own existence, they become implicated themselves— they become part of the community of the concentration camp.

Author Biography

Borowski was born in 1922 to a poor Polish family in what was then part of the Soviet Ukraine. In 1926, Borowski's father, accused of political dissidence, was sent to a labor camp, and when Borowski was eight years old, his mother was sent to Siberia. An aunt then took over the boy's care. In 1932, Borowski's father was freed in a prisoner exchange program between Poland and the Soviet Union, and the two were reunited. Two years later, Borowski's mother rejoined the family in Warsaw.

The young Borowski was educated at a Franciscan boarding school. Borowski was 17 when Poland fell under German occupation at the start of World War II. Schools were closed down, so Borowski studied in underground classes and managed to graduate from secondary school. He then attended the underground Warsaw University, majoring in Polish language and literature. Already a budding writer, Borowski also worked as a stockboy and a night watchman.

In 1942, Borowski printed and distributed his first book of poetry, *Gdziekolwiek ziemia* (translated as *Wherever the Earth*). Borowski anonymously published this collection of metaphoric verse that centered on the death of civilized man in the German labor camps and then distributed it secretly. However, the Gestapo discovered his actions, and within weeks of the volume's release, Borowski and his fiancee, Maria, were arrested. He was sent to several prison camps before arriving at Auschwitz. To ensure his survival, Borowski got a job as an orderly in the camp hospital. As the Allied liberation forces drew close to Auschwitz, Borowski and other prisoners were moved to Dachau. The U.S. Army liberated the camp in May 1945.

Borowski was then transferred to a camp for displaced persons. He left the camp in September to search for his fiancee, whom he had last seen at Birkenau, the women's barracks near Auschwitz. He learned that she was living in Sweden, but he was unable to cross international borders to reach her. Borowski spent a short time in Munich and Paris before returning to Communist Poland in May 1946. His fiancee joined him in November, and they were married the following year.

Following his release, Borowski continued to write stories, including "This Way for the Gas, Ladies and Gentlemen," which he produced at the displaced persons camp. Some of these stories as well as his poetry had been published in Poland before his return. Along with two other Polish Gentile writers, Borowski compiled *We Were in Auschwitz,* stories of life in the concentration camp. The Polish readership, though shocked at the amoral world Borowski depicted, recognized his talent. *Pozegnanie z Maria (Farewell to Maria)* and *Kamienny swiat (World of Stone)* were both published toward the end of the 1940s. These volumes contained Borowski's Auschwitz stories, as well as stories about the displaced person camps in Germany and his return home.

Borowski was wooed by and joined the Communist party in 1948. He turned to writing political propaganda—pro-communist journalistic pieces for Warsaw newspapers. These writings had little literary merit; however, he received a government prize for them. In the summer of 1949, he was sent to Berlin for a year to work in the press section at the Polish Military Mission. He was also given a secret intelligence assignment by the secret police. Less than fifteen months after his return to Poland, in July 1951, Borowski committed suicide.

His five-volume *Utwory zebrane (Collected Works)* was published in Warsaw in 1954. Translations of his works have been published in other countries as well.

Plot Summary

In the barracks of Auschwitz, the unnamed narrator eats his breakfast with Henri, his friend and fellow prisoner. Henri is a member of the so-called Canada squad, members of the Kommando labor gang whose job is to unload the Jewish prisoners from the cattle cars and send them either to the work camp or to the gas chambers. In the midst of their meal, a messenger comes with the news that a transport is arriving. It is the first transport that the camp has seen in several days, and Henri invites the narrator to come work on the ramp. This is how prisoners get food and items of clothing. In the past, the narrator had to depend on Henri for these items, and he accepts the offer.

The narrator and the other workers go to the railroad station. They are joined by SS officers and guards, all of whom wait for the first train to arrive. As the train rounds the bend, the workers all jump to their feet. The train stops on the tracks, alongside the ramp. Anguished cries for water and air can be heard coming from inside. Heads push out through the windows, and bodies pound against the inside of the train. To silence the prisoners, a soldier shoots a volley of rounds into the side of the cattle car. The SS officer warns the workers not to take anything from the Jews beside food.

Then the train doors open. People rush forth from inside. They are ordered to make a pile of their possessions—luggage, blankets, coats, food, money. Some people ask the workers what will happen to them, but the workers, following "camp law," refuse to answer. The Jews are made to go either to the left or the right. Those on the left side board the waiting trucks that will take them to the gas chamber. Those on the right will go to Auschwitz to work. The men carry out the selection quickly, shoving prisoners into the trucks. One SS officer keeps track of how many people have gone to the gas chambers with hash marks.

After the train has been emptied, the prisoner-workers must clean it up. Inside, the narrator finds babies among the filth and squalor. The narrator gives them to an old woman to take to the gas chamber, and she shows her sympathy for him. The narrator suddenly feels very tired. He asks Henri if they are good people; he is concerned because he feels no pity for the Jews.

Once all the people and trucks have gone, the workers collect the Jews' food, as well as the material objects that will go into Germany's coffers. Just as the workers have completed this task, another train rolls in.

Unloading this train, the workers react more brutally and more impatiently. A woman attempts to leave behind her small child, hoping that she will be selected as a laborer. A guard curses her, throwing her on the trucks, and tossing the child in after her. The narrator sees an attractive young woman. She asks the narrator where they are being taken, and when he doesn't answer, she tells him that she knows. She walks off to the truck, though she is young and strong, and her life would have been spared.

After unloading the two transports, the narrator declares to Henri that he is done with this work.

Henri tells him to sit quietly and not let an SS soldier see him. By the light of the stars and the overhead bulbs, the narrator watches the work begin again. He sees a little girl crawl out the window of a train that has just pulled onto the tracks. She walks in circles, stunned and terrified. An SS man kicks her down and then shoots her with his revolver. The narrator goes back to the ramp to work, but when he touches yet another corpse, he vomits.

Leaning against the stack of rails, the narrator dreams of being back at his bunk. He longs to return to the camp, which is a place of peace compared to the hell he is now in. Then, finally, the last transport has been unloaded. The dead are cleared off the ramp. The prisoners line up to go back to camp, weighted down with the food belonging to the Jews.

Characters

Andrei

Andrei is a Russian sailor who is a member of the labor gang that unloads the Jews from the cattle cars. He attacks a woman who is trying to deny her child to keep from being sent to the gas chambers. Through his act of attacking the woman, he wins the approval of the SS officers.

Girl

The narrator notices an attractive, confident Jewish girl. She calmly asks him what will happen to them. Though he will not answer her, she tells him that she already knows the truth. Instead of allowing herself to be among the women chosen to go to the labor camp, she puts herself on the trucks headed for the gas chambers.

Henri

Henri, a Communist from France, is a friend of the narrator's. A member of the Canada labor gang, Henri regularly smuggles back food and clothing for his friends. He has a cynical attitude toward the camp, his fellow prisoners, and the Jewish victims, as well as a clear understanding that the welfare of the prisoner-workers depends on the continuing destruction of the Jews.

Little Girl

The little girl pushes herself out of the train window. Her mind has been unhinged by the experience, and she walks in circles until an SS man knocks her down with a kick and then shoots her dead.

Narrator

The unnamed narrator is a Polish gentile imprisoned in Auschwitz. He is better off than most prisoners, receiving food packages from his family. His trip to the ramp is the first time he has worked such duty. On his way to the train station, he considers himself lucky to get this work detail because he knows he will be rewarded with food. However, he does not anticipate the horror of the work: forcing the Jews from the cattle cars, fending off their questions of what will happen to them, cleaning out the cars of the human detriment and dead babies. After unloading his first transport, the narrator feels tired and nauseous, yet completely disassociated from himself. Instead of feeling pity for the Jews, he is furious with them because, as he rationalizes it, if the Nazis were not determined to murder them, he would not be forced to carry out this disturbing and dehumanizing work. As a response to his malaise, he loses control, unloading the second train with barely restrained brutality; he wants the Jews to be gone so he is not reminded of what he is doing. After working on two transports, he is unable to continue. Instead, he longs only to return to the peace that the concentration camp provides where at least he remains among the living and not in continual contact with those who are like the waking dead.

Themes

The Holocaust and Its Literature

The term *Holocaust* refers to the genocide of European Jews and others by the Nazis during World War II. The narrator of "This Way for the Gas, Ladies and Gentlemen" is a prisoner at the infamous Auschwitz, one of the death camps where the brutal killings were carried out. Around six million Jews died in the Holocaust, along with at least three million prisoners of other backgrounds. The Nazis organized this mass extermination with extreme efficiency; for example, by the end of the day that the story takes place, 15,000 people have been sent almost effortlessly to their deaths.

"This Way for the Gas, Ladies and Gentlemen" is one of several of Borowski's Auschwitz stories and part of a larger genre of Holocaust literature. Writers such as Primo Levi and Elie Wiesel have produced some of the most famous accounts of survivor testimony. Holocaust literature focuses on how people survived amidst the horror of the concentration camps. Different Holocaust survivors have posited different explanations. One leading view, proposed by Viktor Frankl, states that in spite of terrible circumstances, the prisoners still found life to be unconditionally meaningful, even in its suffering. Other survivors support the idea that there was no real meaning to the death camps, that to survive people had to leave behind all their notions of the "normal world" and normal human behavior; Borowski's work falls into the latter category.

Death and Survival

Death and survival are inextricably linked in "This Way for the Gas, Ladies and Gentlemen." For the narrator (and the other prisoners in his situation) to stay alive, he must take part in the business of the camp, which primarily revolves around the murder of the Jews and other "undesirables." The narrator must carry out jobs that facilitate the destruction of the "cremo" transports, be it actually unloading the Jews—as in the story—or some other camp-related job (as Borowski performed in real life). The physical welfare of the prisoners also depends on the destruction of the Jews. Prisoner-workers get necessary items, from clothing to food, from the prisoners who are sent to their death. As the story opens, the prisoners are feeling the effects of the recent lack of transports arriving at the camp. As Henri notes, if the camp "runs out of people" to kill, he and his fellow prisoners will starve to death. "All of us live on what they bring," he says, underscoring the connection between death and survival. Indeed, when the narrator leaves the barracks to attend to the transport—his first time doing so—he considers himself lucky. In aiding in the deaths of others, he will facilitate his own survival.

Morality

In the world of the camp, traditional notions of morality have no meaning. The narrator and his fellow prisoners rely on the deaths of others for their survival, so they are thus implicated in the murder of the Jews. What is more troubling, the prisoners are forced to take part in carrying out this crime; if they were to refuse to do their jobs, they would be killed themselves. To exist under such circumstances, the narrator is forced to detach himself mentally and emotionally from his actions. The narrator refers to the arrival of the cattle cars as the camp's "usual diversion," thereby equating the death of thousands of innocent people with entertainment. He speaks casually of letting a praying rabbi continue "raving" because the Nazis would "take him to the oven that much sooner." The only kindness the prisoners show those who are doomed to the gas chambers is deceiving them about their impending fate; the prisoners tell the Jews they don't know where they are being taken.

The narrator raises moral issues at the ramp when he asks Henri if they are good people. Instead of feeling pity for the doomed Jews, he is furious with them—because of these people, he thinks, he is forced to be at the ramp at Auschwitz, experiencing this horror. Despite his rhetoric, however, the narrator demonstrates physical signs of his moral turmoil. He feels nauseous, until eventually, after unloading several transports, he loses control and vomits. As he sits down, he suddenly "see[s] the camp as a haven of peace," which shows how far from the mainstream he has traveled; in the abnormal world of Auschwitz, the death camp has become a refuge.

Topics for Further Study

- Imagine that you are a journalist writing about life in Auschwitz. Write an article using Borowski's story as your reference source.

- Read other survivor accounts and compare these former prisoners' stories and experiences to Borowski's. What similarities do you find? What differences do you note?

- Write a monologue that one of the Jewish characters in the story might have given at the ramp. What aspects would you focus on? How would you portray his feelings?

- Who do you think has a more realistic way of looking at camp life, the narrator or his friend Andrei? Explain your answer.

- Imagine that you are a Jew who had survived the Holocaust. Write your response to Borowski's story.

- Do you think Borowski's story implies his own feelings about what took place in Auschwitz? Explain your answer.

Style

Point-of-View

Although the story is written from the first-person point-of-view, the unnamed narrator maintains a tone of extreme detachment from the horrific events that surround him and in which he participates. He reports the goings-on in a casual, unin-volved manner, so that his observations—both those made to himself and to others—resemble nothing as much as those of an impartial journalist. For example, although Henri complains about a Jewish man's wailing prayers, the narrator points out in a practical, unconcerned manner that the unpleasant noise will only lead the Nazis to gas the rabbi that much sooner. Despite the narrator's distant attitude, he is touched by the horror of the ramp. His nausea and his eventual refusal to take part in further unloading show that his distance stems not from a lack of feeling; instead, it emerges as a coping mechanism.

Still, the narrator's understatement of the events of Auschwitz is disconcerting and continually keeps the reader off-balance. The second line of the story is a good example of the power of Borowski's technique: "The delousing is finally over, and our striped suits are back from the tanks of Cyclone B solution, an efficient killer of lice in clothing and of men in gas chambers."

Symbolism and Metaphor

"This Way for the Gas, Ladies and Gentlemen" is rich with symbolism and metaphor. In this base world, where survival is all that matters, people become animals—Nazi captors and prisoners alike. The Nazis have "beefy" faces. A female SS officer with a "rat-like" smile "sniffs around" the ramp. Another officer complains that the prisoner-workers, stunned by the events, are "standing about like sheep," and he whips them like the beasts of burden they have become. The starving Greek prisoners on transport duty, who are desperate enough to eat rotted, mildewed food, are looked upon as pigs, *schweinedreck,* and "huge human insects" with jaws pumping greedily. Even the trucks that participate in the slaughter transform into "mad dogs."

The Jewish victims are not spared such degrading comparisons either. A couple locked in a frantic last embrace are "dragged like cattle" to the waiting truck; children run wildly around the ramp "howling like dogs." The dead babies retrieved from the cattle cars are bloated monsters, which the prisoners carry out "like chickens, holding several in each hand." A corpse is referred to simply as a "mound of meat."

The oppressive heat, which the narrator describes as "unbearable," is also important symbolically. It is a constant physical reminder of the crematoria where the bodies of the dead are burned. The breeze in the air brings no relief, but instead, "feels like a sizzling blast from a furnace." The heat is also trapped in the cattle cars, which the narrator describes as "an inferno." Auschwitz is a very real hell, both for those who work there and those who are sent there to die.

Setting

The story takes place at Auschwitz, the Nazi concentration camp where the largest number of European Jews were killed. Auschwitz was both a labor camp where thousands of prisoners lived (Auschwitz I) and a death camp with gas chambers and crematoria where more than a million people were sent to their deaths (Auschwitz II). The two camps were located about a mile and a half apart, and each was heavily guarded, surrounded by gates and watchtowers. At the ramp, as the prisoners disembark from the cattle cars, they are immediately sent either to the right—to labor in the camps— or to the left—to death in the gas chambers.

The area around the ramp resembles a smalltown railway station, with a square surrounded by chestnut trees that provide a bit of shade in the heat. Although the narrator initially describes it as "cheerful" looking, the guards posted all along the rails— and their violent actions—allow little opportunity for him to maintain this facade of normalcy. Soon the ramp transforms into what it really is: a hellish place of murder and madness.

Historical Context

Poland Under Attack

Despite being a dominant power in Eastern Europe from the fourteenth to the seventeenth century, in the eighteenth century, Poland was divided up by its neighbors. With the end of World War I and the Treaty of Versailles, however, an independent Polish state was formed. Poland also received a large area of German territory, including the Polish Corridor. This strip of territory separated Germany from East Prussia, which gave Poland access to the Baltic Sea. The seaport Danzig, to which Germany retained usage rights, became a free city administered by the League of Nations. Poland's post-World War I government was precarious, however, and its leaders were unable to conclude defensive security agreements with other European powers.

As German expansion in Europe grew, Poland's government vainly attempted to protect itself. Danzig had a large German population, and Adolf Hitler eventually claimed it for Germany. A strong Nazi Party developed in Danzig, and by 1937, it controlled the city government. These officials made relations with Poland increasingly difficult.

In August 1939, Germany and the Soviet Union announced a pact of non-aggression in which each nation pledged it would never attack the other. Also called the Hitler-Stalin Pact, this pact included a secret agreement to divide Eastern Europe between the two nations; Germany would take western Poland and the Soviet Union would take eastern Poland in addition to other nearby territory. Within a week of signing this pact, Hitler demanded that Danzig be returned to Germany and that the Germans be allowed to occupy a strip running through the Polish Corridor.

Compare & Contrast

- **1930s:** The avant-garde is influential among leading writers. Witold Gombrowicz, who moved to Argentina in 1939, gains an international reputation.

  Today: With the ending of censorship in 1989, the works of Polish writers like Jerzy Kosinski are available to Polish readers for the first time. In 1996, Wislawa Szymborska becomes the second Polish poet to win the Nobel Prize for literature.

- **1940s:** In 1939, the Polish population is 35 million, including sizable Jewish, German, Ukrainian, and Belorussian minorities. During World War II, more than 6 million Poles lose their lives. Polish Jewry is largely destroyed. Most of the Germans in western Poland are expelled, and the Ukrainian and Belorussian populations are transferred to the Soviet Union.

Today: Poland's population stands at just over 38.5 million. Of this, 98 percent are ethnic Poles.

- **1940s:** On the eve of World War II, Poland is ruled by a "Government of Generals." During the war, the Polish government goes into exile, and Poland comes under foreign rule. After World War II, Poland is re-established as a Soviet satellite state and adopts a Communist government.

  Today: Poland has been a parliamentary democracy since 1989 and practices a market economy.

- **1940s:** Anywhere from 1 to 3 million are put to death by the Nazis at the concentration camp Auschwitz.

  Today: The remains of Auschwitz are a UNESCO World Heritage Site. A museum and memorial, first created in 1947, are on the site of the former Nazi concentration camp.

- **1940s:** The Nazis murder at least 9

million people during the Holocaust.

Today: In Rwanda, in 1994, the Hutu-led government systematically kills between 750,000 to 1 million Tutsi and moderate Hutu.

On September 1, 1939, Hitler declared the annexation of Danzig to the Third Reich. At the same time and without warning, the German air force and ground armies launched a massive attack on Poland from three directions: the north, south, and west. Poland's military was unprepared for this blitzkrieg, or "lightning war." Then, on September 17, Soviet forces invaded Poland from the east. Within a month, Poland had surrendered.

An Occupied Poland

As had happened many times in its history, Poland disappeared from the maps of Europe. The nation was divided between the victors. The western half of Poland, occupied by the Nazis, was declared a new territory, the "General Government," while the eastern half was incorporated into the Soviet Union. Both the German and Soviet governments committed mass executions of civilians, political leaders, and military officers; arrested thousands of political prisoners; initiated police screening and registration; and segregated the population according to categories of undesirability.

Hitler had the goal of obliterating all traces of

Polish history and culture. By October 1939, many Poles had been stripped of all rights. The use of the Polish language was forbidden; secondary schools were closed; and young men were drafted into the German army. The Gestapo forced about two million Jews to relocate to ghettos. The Soviets also carried out atrocities. All Poles living within Soviet territory were declared Soviet citizens. The Soviets deported some two million Poles to Kazakhstan, Siberia, and the Soviet Far East, took over Polish businesses and factories, destroyed churches, and closed savings accounts.

In 1941, Germany attacked the Soviet Union and captured eastern Poland. The Germans' New Order in Poland included plans to Germanize suitable Poles and relocate the rest beyond the Ural Mountains; enslave the Slavs; and exterminate inferior or useless human beings. The Soviets began to organize Polish armies for their own defense, joined forces with the Allies, and began its advance on the Eastern Front, or eastern Poland, in 1943. In August 1944, Polish resistance fighters in Warsaw rose up against German occupation forces. Stalin ordered his troops that were approaching the city to halt, giving the Nazis time to smash the Polish forces and eliminated any potential competitors to Stalin's hand-picked communist government.

Concentration Camps

Along with Jews, leaders (religious, educational, and political) and many others were imprisoned and put to death at the concentration camps. Other Poles were executed in public. The first mass execution of World War II took place on December 27, 1939, and was a strategy of war, aimed at terrorizing Poles into subservience.

Auschwitz, located in southern Poland outside of Cracow, remains perhaps the most infamous concentration camp. For the first 21 months of its existence, Auschwitz was primarily inhabited by Polish non-Jews; by the time of the camp's liberation, more than 100,000 non-Jewish Poles had died at Auschwitz. However, soon it became a final destination point for Jews from throughout Europe, who were sent there in cattle cars and gassed. In 1945, as the Allies were approaching, the Nazis exterminated more than 400,000 Jews. That summer the Nazis began to evacuate the inmates of Auschwitz into Germany.

Communist Poland

During the war, a free Polish government-in-exile had been based in London. However, after the war, Soviet dictator Joseph Stalin refused to recognize this government. The United States and Great Britain wanted a democratic government in Poland. Stalin agreed that an unspecified number of pro-Western Poles would be granted a place in the new government and reluctantly agreed to hold free elections in Poland, but he did not say when. Over the protests of the Western Allies, Stalin installed a pro-Soviet Communist government in Poland.

Stalin also insisted that the Soviet Union would retain the Polish territories it had seized in September 1939, but was not willing to risk war over this demand. The Soviets were able to crush all opposition. In 1956, however, Polish protestors began insisting on greater rights and threatened to revolt. The Soviets allowed Wladyslaw Gomulka, a former Polish leader deposed by Stalin for wanting to bring Poland more independence, to return to the country. Under Gomulka, who remained in power for fourteen years, Poland gained a small amount of independence in domestic policy-making.

Critical Overview

Borowski's story "This Way for the Gas, Ladies and Gentlemen" first appeared in Poland the spring of 1946, little more than a year after the Nazis began evacuating Auschwitz's more than 50,000 prisoners (including Borowski). The story was included in the 1947 volume, *We Were in Auschwitz,* which collected short pieces by Borowski along with the works of fellow Poles Janusz Nel Siedlecki and Krystyn Olszewski. In their collective Preface, the authors explained that they hoped to talk "without subterfuge, openly" about the horrors they saw in Auschwitz. Their publication was an early attempt to diminish the already developing legend of the concentration camp: that in this place of horror, heroism supplanted cowardice, and prisoners worked together for the good of their fellow sufferers.

Two years later, Borowski's first collection, also titled *This Way for the Gas, Ladies and Gentlemen,* was published in Poland, making Borowski one of the first writers to depict the harshness of the concentration camps. Borowski's earliest readers noticed what became one of the most unique features of his stories: that no one was the "victim" and no one was the "criminal." Rather, the narrator in his stories is part of the concentration camp community, which shares in the collective guilt over the deaths of millions of Europeans. Immediately, Borowski drew criticism; the Catholic

Church denounced his nihilism while the Polish Communist party condemned his work as decadent, Americanized, and amoral.

In 1967, an English translation of *This Way for the Gas, Ladies and Gentlemen* was published, and American critics in numerous publications immediately responded favorably to Borowski's courageous message. George Eckstein of *Dissent* noted that the stories were "remarkable in the unsentimental, unflinching frankness with which they face the universal brutality." Rather than eliding over the prisoners' role in the deaths of millions of people, Borowski emphasizes their brutality and implied guilt because this was the "bitter essence of life in the Nazi concentration camp."

Daniel Stern of the *New York Times Book Review* reserved the highest of praise for Borowski, whom he compared to noted Holocaust writer Elie Wiesel. "Do not let the title of this short-story collection mislead you," he admonished readers, cautioning them from believing the book to be "merely another of the reports from hell" that reached readers in the decades after the Holocaust. "It is a true work of art, full of brutality and pain. . . . [Borowski] paints a picture of the horror and madness that ruled the concentration camps, so brilliantly that the immediacy of the experience is almost too much to bear." Stern further singled out the title story as a "bitterly perfect portrayal of the 'politics' of camp life," which requires prisoners to be pitted against other prisoners. Borowski's skill, wrote Stern, causes the reader to momentarily lose all "normal moral control" and root for the narrator. He also lauded the scenes of Jews arriving at the camp as "impossible to forget."

This Way for the Gas, Ladies and Gentlemen was reissued in 1976, as part of a series of literature from Eastern Europe. Again, it drew overwhelmingly favorable criticism. Even thirty years later, wrote A. Alvarez in *The New York Times Book Review,* Borowski's prose still had an "impact and power [that is] as unsettling now as it must have been then."

In addition to responding to Borowski's message, literary critics have responded to his style. Stern praised Borowski's "irony tempered with lyricism." Alvarez compared Borowski's prose, the "purity of style and language" to that of Ernest Hemingway's, "which remained even while expressing the fiercest corruption." He continued, "There is no melodrama, no moral gesturing. He [Borowski] simply records the facts, lucidly, in a style as stripped and deprived as the fact themselves."

Because of this style, some critics have found Borowski's work more akin to documentary or nonfiction than short fiction. Mark Shechner wrote for the *Nation* that Borowski's stories in *This Way for the Gas, Ladies and Gentlemen* are "barely transformed autobiographical sketches. . . They are fiction only in a formal sense." He praised Borowski's detached style ofwriting as doing "what is morally required," which is allowing the depravity of the Holocaust "to speak for itself." Indeed, Irving Howe wrote in a lengthy *New Republic* piece on Holocaust literature that while Borowski's detached tone "in a naturalistic novel would signal moral revulsion from represented ugliness, it has here become a condition of survival." Unlike many previous critics, however, Howe only responded to Borowski's "testimony." For Howe, the stories' very authenticity rendered him "all but indifferent to their status as art."

Literary critics have continued to explicate Borowski's work. In a 1982 essay, Lawrence Langer asked "[W]hat are we to make of Borowski's narrator, who helps drive victims from the cattle cars, unloads their belongings, watches them being led off to the gas chambers?" The narrator, answered Langer, lived in a world of "choiceless choice," for he "is left only a choice between evils, between extermination and continued existence in Auschwitz."

In 2000, *We Were in Auschwitz* was published for the first time in English, and Borowski's work has continued to elicit strong reactions. Despite the fact that more than half a century has elapsed since Borowski first wrote about Auschwitz, the reviewer for *Publishers Weekly* experienced the book's "chilling immediacy." In keeping with earlier critics, this reviewer found the volume to be "an important addition to Holocaust studies, but not for those who choose to see survival in Auschwitz as a triumph of the human spirit."

What Do I Read Next?

- *Bread for the Deported* (translated into English in 1997) by Bogdan Wojdowski is a novel about World War II Poland, describing the terrible difficulties of life in the Warsaw ghetto and culminating in deportation to the Treblinka concentration camp.

- Auschwitz survivor Ilona Karmel wrote the novel *An Estate of Memory* (1969) comparing the experiences of three women in the camp.

- Czeslaw Milosz, the Nobel Prize winner for Literature in 1980, wrote the political poem, "On the Death of Tadeusz Borowski."

- Primo Levi's *Survival in Auschwitz*

(1947) is one of the classic accounts of life in Nazi concentration camps.
- *Night* (1958) by Elie Wiesel is a semi-autobiographical account of a young boy's spiritual reaction to Auschwitz.

Sources

Alvarez, A., "The Victim of a Full European Education," in *New York Times Book Review,* February 29, 1976, pp. 3-4.

Eckstein, George, "The Festering Sore," in *Dissent,* Vol. 247, No. 2, March-April, 1968, pp. 184-86.

Howe, Irving, "Writing and the Holocaust," in *New Republic,* October 27, 1986, p. 27.

Kott, Jan, Introduction to *This Way for the Gas, Ladies and Gentlemen,* by Tadeusz Borowski, translated by Barbara Vedder, Penguin Books, 1976.

Langer, Lawrence L., "Auschwitz: The Death of Choice," in *Versions of Survival: The Holocaust and the Human Spirit,* State University of New York Press, 1982, pp. 67-129.

Review in *Publishers Weekly,* Vol. 247, No. 23, June 5, 2000.

Shechner, Mark, "Survival Declined," in *Nation,* Vol. 222, No. 24, June 19, 1976, pp. 760-62.

Siedlecki, Janusz, Krystyn Olszewski, Tadeusz Borowski, and Anatol Girs, Preface to *We Were in Auschwitz,* Welcome Rain Publishers, 2000.

Stern, Daniel, "Making Way for the Dead," in *New York Times Book Review,* November 19, 1967, p. 81.

Wirth, Andrzej, "A Discovery of Tragedy," in *Polish Review,* translated by Adam Czerniawski, Vol. 12, No. 3, Summer 1967, pp. 42-52.

Further Reading

Aroneanu, Eugene, comp., *Inside the Concentration Camps,* translated by Thomas Whissen, Praeger, 1996.

> This oral history presents 100 eyewitness testimonies, first recorded in 1945, of the concentration experience from the point of view of many different types of survivors.

Borowski, Tadeusz, *This Way for the Gas, Ladies and Gentlemen,* translated by Barbara Vedder, Penguin USA, 1992.

> This is a recent edition of Borowski's work.

Clendinnen, Inga, *Reading the Holocaust,* Cambridge University Press, 1999.

> Clendinnen explores the experience of the Holocaust from the point of view of both the victims and the perpetrators, and discusses survivor testimonies of writers.

Gutman, Yisrael, and Michael Berenbaum, eds., *Anatomy of the Auschwitz Death Camp,* Indiana University Press, 1998.

> The book compiles reports from 27 multinational contributors on the

history, population, and operations of Auschwitz.

Hatley, James, *Suffering Witness: The Quandary of Responsibility after the Irreparable,* State University of New York Press, 2000.

> Hatley uses survivor literature, including works of This book presents an overview of Polish life under Borowski, and philosophy to argue that bearing wit-the German occupation, focusing on such aspects as ness to the Holocaust is a serious responsibility. the government, the underground, and daily life.

Lukas, Richard C, and Norman Davies, *The Forgotten* Marrus, Michael R., *The Holocaust in History,* Penguin *Holocaust: The Poles under German Occupation 1939-1944,* Books, 1987. 2d rev. ed., Hippocrene Books, 1997.

> This book presents an overview of Polish life under the German occupation, focusing on such aspects as the government, the underground, and daily life.

Marrus, Michael R., The *Holocaust in History*, Penguin Books, 1987.

> Marrus discusses the Holocaust.

www.ingramcontent.com/pod-product-compliance
Ingram Content Group UK Ltd.
Pitfield, Milton Keynes, MK11 3LW, UK
UKHW020724250225
4746UKWH00042B/463

9 781375 394765